Pebble®

Horses

American Paint Horses

by Kim O'Brien

Consulting Editor: Gail Saunders-Smith, PhD

Capstone press®

Mankato, Minnesota

Pebble Books are published by Capstone Press,
151 Good Counsel Drive, P.O. Box 669, Mankato, Minnesota 56002.
www.capstonepress.com

1 2 3 4 5 6 14 13 12 11 10 09

Library of Congress Cataloging-in-Publication Data
O'Brien, Kim.
American paint horses / by Kim O'Brien.
    p. cm. — (Pebble books. Horses)
    Includes bibliographical references and index.
    Summary: "A brief introduction to the characteristics, life cycle, and uses of the
American paint horse breed" — Provided by publisher.
    ISBN-13: 978-1-4296-2231-8 (hardcover)
    ISBN-10: 1-4296-2231-8 (hardcover)
    1. American paint horse — Juvenile literature. I. Title.
SF293.A47O27 2009
636.1'3 — dc22   2008026824

Note to Parents and Teachers

The Horses set supports national science standards related to life science. This book describes and illustrates American paint horses. The images support early readers in understanding the text. The repetition of words and phrases helps early readers learn new words. This book also introduces early readers to subject-specific vocabulary words, which are defined in the Glossary section. Early readers may need assistance to read some words and to use the Table of Contents, Glossary, Read More, Internet Sites, and Index sections of the book.

Table of Contents

Splashed with Paint

The American paint horse's coat looks like it has been splashed with paint. This horse breed is known for its colorful coat patterns.

tobiano coat

6

Tobiano and overo are the two main coat patterns. A tobiano paint horse has patches of white hair that cross over its back.

On an overo horse,
patches of white do not
cross over its back.
Overo horses have at least
one dark leg.

From Foal to Adult

American paint foals are
born with patches of color.
The patches might become
darker or lighter
as the foal grows.

withers

Paint horses are fully grown
in about four years.
They stand between
14 and 17 hands high.

Horses are measured in hands.
Each hand is 4 inches (10 centimeters).
A horse is measured from the ground
to its withers.

A Horse for Everyone

People enjoy riding paints.
They are calm horses.

Some owners show
their paint horses
in western riding events.
Western riders wear
cowboy hats and boots.

Paints compete in jumping
events in horse shows.
The horses are steady
and willing jumpers.

American paint horses
have beautiful coats
and a gentle nature.
All kinds of owners enjoy
these colorful horses.

Glossary

breed — a group of animals that come from common relatives

coat — the hair covering a horse's body

foal — a young horse

nature — an animal's personality

overo — a solid coat color with white markings that don't cross over the horse's back; one or more of the legs on an overo horse is dark.

steady — firm and not shaky

tobiano — a solid coat color with white markings that cross over the horse's back; all four legs of a tobiano horse are white below the knees.

western riding — a style of horseback riding first created by Spanish and American cowboys in the western United States

Read More

Van Cleaf, Kristin. *American Paint Horses.* Horses. Set II. Edina, Minn.: Abdo, 2006.

Pitts, Zachary. *The Pebble First Guide to Horses.* Pebble First Guides. Mankato, Minn.: Capstone Press, 2009.

Internet Sites

FactHound offers a safe, fun way to find educator-approved Internet sites related to this book.

Here's what you do:

1. Visit *www.facthound.com*
2. Choose your grade level.
3. Begin your search.

This book's ID number is 9781429622318.

FactHound will fetch the best sites for you!

Index

Word Count: 162
Grade: 1
Early-Intervention Level: 18

Editorial Credits
Erika L. Shores, editor; Bobbi J. Wyss, designer;
    Sarah L. Schuette, photo shoot direction

Photo Credits
All photos by Capstone Press/TJ Thoraldson Digital Photography, except pages 6
    and 18, Shutterstock/Margo Harrison

The Capstone Press Photo Studio thanks Debbie Attenberger and Cedar Ridge
Arabians for their help with photo shoots.

Capstone Press thanks Robert Coleman, PhD, associate professor of
Equine Extension at the University of Kentucky, Lexington's Department
of Animal Sciences, for reviewing this book.